Mitchellville
Elementary Library

THE ANTARCTIC OCEAN

ANTARCTICA

Lynn M. Stone

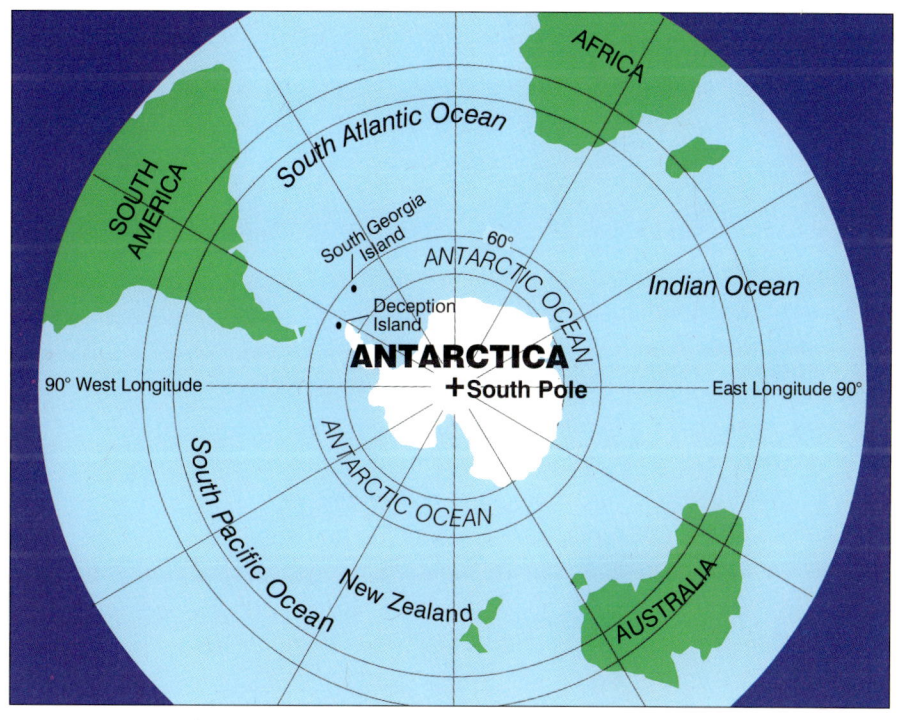

The Rourke Book Co., Inc.
Vero Beach, Florida 32964

© 1995 The Rourke Book Co., Inc.

All rights reserved. No part of this book may be reproduced or utilized in any form or by any means, electronic or mechanical including photocopying, recording or by any information storage and retrieval system without permission in writing from the publisher.

PHOTO CREDITS
All photos © Lynn M. Stone except pages 17 and 18 © John N. Heine

Library of Congress Cataloging-in-Publication Data

Stone, Lynn M.
    The Antarctic Ocean / by Lynn M. Stone.
        p. cm. — (Antarctica)
    Includes index.
    ISBN 1-55916-138-8
    1. Antarctic Ocean—Juvenile literature.   [1. Antarctic Ocean]
I. Title II. Series: Stone, Lynn M.   Antarctica.
GC461.S76 1995
551.46' 9—dc20   95–5984
                                                    CIP
                                                      AC

Printed in the USA

TABLE OF CONTENTS

The Antarctic Ocean	5
The Stormy Antarctic	6
Ocean Ice	9
Icebergs	11
A Rich Ocean	14
Marine Animals	16
Life in the Antarctic Ocean	19
Living in the Antarctic Ocean	20
Birds and Mammals	22
Glossary	23
Index	24

THE ANTARCTIC OCEAN

The frozen continent of Antarctica lies at the bottom of the southern half of the world. This huge, ice-capped mass of land is surrounded by the Antarctic Ocean.

The Antarctic Ocean is very cold. Close to Antarctica itself, the ocean temperature is below the freezing point—32 degrees Fahrenheit. However, salt in the water keeps some of the ocean from freezing.

Beneath the ocean surface are great undersea mountains and canyons, some as deep as five miles.

The icy Antarctic Ocean rings the great white continent

THE STORMY ANTARCTIC

For an American traveling toward Antarctica, the Antarctic Ocean begins about 200 miles south of Cape Horn. Cape Horn is the southern tip of South America.

The Antarctic Ocean is often roughed up by storms. Dark clouds drift over a black, tossing sea. Seabirds skim over mighty waves that make passing ships rock and roll and shake and shudder.

Closer to Antarctica, the sea is calmer. This is the quiet world of pack ice.

Storm waves lash the bow of a ship in the Antarctic Ocean

OCEAN ICE

Pack ice begins to form each March with the start of the Antarctic winter. Extremely cold air turns much of the upper layer of ocean water into floating pieces of ice. These chunks and "pancakes" of ice slowly squeeze, or pack, together as they grow.

By winter's end in late September, the ice ring around Antarctica is as large as the continent itself! Most of the sea ice melts away during the Antarctic summer.

Pack ice breaks up with the longer, warmer days of Antarctic spring and summer

ICEBERGS

Icebergs float in the Antarctic Ocean like frozen ships. Each iceberg is a different size and shape from the others. The biggest are more than 60 miles long and 40 miles wide!

Icebergs begin as land ice. As ice inches slowly from land into the sea, pieces break off and become icebergs.

The average iceberg lasts about four years. Sooner or later, it floats northward to warmer water and melts.

Even without tickets, penguins can hitch a ride on an iceberg

On days stormy or still, long-winged ocean birds, like this albatross, skim over Antarctic seas

Wonderfully weird, a bloodless ice fish lies aboard a Russian research ship in the Antarctic Ocean

A RICH OCEAN

The Antarctic Ocean is surprisingly rich with **marine** (muh REEN), or sea, life. Seabirds, seals and whales are plentiful. These large animals live by eating smaller marine animals.

The Antarctic Ocean is especially rich because it is cold and high in **minerals** (MIN er uhlz). Cold ocean water is better than warm for the growth of tiny marine plants.

Many millions of Antarctic seabirds, nearly half of them penguins, live on the marine life of the Antarctic Ocean

MARINE ANIMALS

These tiny marine plants, together with tiny marine animals, are called **plankton** (PLANK ton). They float freely in the ocean, especially in the upper layer of water.

Plankton share the Antarctic Ocean with larger marine animals, such as sea urchins, starfish, squids, sponges, snails, octopuses, fish, seals, whales and seabirds. All these Antarctic animals have cousins in warmer seas.

Red sea stars wait for scraps while hungry nemertean worms crawl over a dead marine animal on the Antarctic Ocean bottom

LIFE IN THE ANTARCTIC OCEAN

    Plankton helps make it possible for the large Antarctic animals to live. One of the most important plankton creatures is the Antarctic krill. The shrimplike krill eats smaller members of the plankton "stew."

    Fish, whales, seals and penguins, in turn, dine on millions of krill. Krill has also become an important food for people in Japan.

The long "arms" of an Antarctic Ocean sea anemone trap a jellyfish as sea spiders gather around for leftovers

LIVING IN THE ANTARCTIC OCEAN

How can any creature live in water with a temperature below freezing? Antarctic animals have solved the problem.

Drivers prevent auto engines from freezing by adding anti-freeze chemicals to them. Antarctic Ocean animals produce their own anti-freeze chemicals!

Birds and mammals of the sea help protect themselves from cold air and water with a layer of fat called **blubber** (BLUH ber). Birds also stay warm thanks to a dense coat of feathers.

Seals, like whales, depend upon a thick layer of blubber to stay warm in icy seas

BIRDS AND MAMMALS

For the great whales the sea is a permanent home. Antarctica's six **species** (SPEE sheez), or kinds, of seals leave the ocean only to rest and raise their pups.

Seabirds—petrels, albatrosses, penguins—feed on and in the Antarctic Ocean. Sometimes these birds remain at sea for weeks or even months.

Each spring the seabirds gather in seaside bird "villages" called **colonies** (KAH luh neez). There they raise their chicks, feeding them food from the Antarctic Ocean.

Glossary

blubber (BLUH ber) — a layer of fat which helps keep animals warm in cold climates

colony (KAH luh nee) — a group of animals of the same kind living together, especially to nest or raise young

marine (muh REEN) — of or relating to the sea

mineral (MIN er uhl) — any one of some 3,000 solid, non-living materials found in nature

plankton (PLANK ton) — tiny, floating plants and animals of the seas and other bodies of water

species (SPEE sheez) — a certain kind of animal within a closely related group; for example, a *blue* whale

INDEX

animals   14, 16, 19, 20
Antarctic Ocean   5, 6, 11, 14,
    16, 22
    life of   14
    temperature of   5
blubber   20
canyons   5
Cape Horn   6
fish   16, 19
ice   6, 9
icebergs   11
krill   19

minerals   14
mountains   5
penguins   19, 22
plankton   16, 19
plants   14
seabirds   6, 14, 16, 22
seals   14, 16, 19, 22
storms   6
summer   9
waves   6
whales   14, 16, 19, 22
winter   9